POLITICS AND CULTURE

POLITICS AND CULTURE

A CHRISTIAN PERSPECTIVE

RICK THOMAS

POLITICS AND CULTURE:
A Christian Perspective

ISBN 978-1-966741-12-1

Rick Thomas

Edited by Sheron Wallace

Life Over Coffee
8595 Pelham Rd Ste 400 #406,
Greenville, SC 29615
LifeOverCoffee.com

The Great Commission
Go therefore and make disciples of all nations,
baptizing them in the name of the Father and of the
Son and of the Holy Spirit, teaching them to observe
all that I have commanded you. And behold, I am with
you always, to the end of the age.
(Matthew 28:19-20)

For additional resources, visit
lifeovercoffee.com

Table of Contents

Preface

Someone asked me why I share political messages on my personal social media accounts. He then followed up by saying that politics stink. It was not one of those "stay in your lane" questions as much as it was a curious onlooker, a fellow Christian thinking about their role in the political arena. His question is worth exploring, and every Christian who wants to make a difference in their sphere should evaluate their role in politics and culture.

The Bible Says

The most obvious response to why I share political and cultural messages on my social media platforms is because the Bible does not forbid it, which is not a blanket edict that suggests, "If the Bible does not forbid it, then it's fair game." However, there are no Scriptures that prohibit a believer from engaging in politics, culture, sports, economics, or any other discipline and vocation that is part of how we live in God's world.

Each believer has to determine at what level they want to engage in their world. Engagement or non-engagement is not necessarily sinful, though we must purpose in our hearts what is appropriate for us to do. The aromatic nature of politics should not be the overruling indicator in our decision-making process. Many things stink, and it's precisely because of this sad reality in a fallen world that we should bring the aroma of Christ to many matters that impact all of us—including politics. Actual or potential messiness should not be prohibitive regarding a person's political, social, or cultural engagement.

Some people say the church stinks, which is true—in part, and they use it as an excuse not to be part of a local gathering. Others think similarly about the messiness of a person's life, using an individual's unique Adamic fallenness to refrain from obeying the Great Commission or the many one-another passages in the New Testament. The world stinks. What would you expect (John 11:39; Job 19:17)? If unpleasantness were the most vital thing about moving forward with political, social, or cultural engagement, there would be no scandalous gospel (Hebrews 12:1-2).

Salt and Light

The better question for each Christian to respond to is what is an effective way to be salt and light in our fallen world as we spread the fame of God near and far (Matthew 5:13-16; 1 Corinthians 10:31). Everyone has a sphere of influence, and there is no question that God calls us to share the message of Christ to the world, whether that is our children, cul-de-sac, community, or country. Unfortunately, some Christians believe their responsibility for sharing the message of Christ is for evangelistic purposes only.

A segment of that group has a tight definition of how to do that: giving a Bible tract to a stranger, the beginning and end of their Great Commission endeavors. Others believe that religion and politics should never mix, which is improbable because we cannot segregate our ontology (state of being: who we are at our core) from what we do and where we do it. It would be like asking Christ to stop being Christ when He stepped into political contexts or conversations.

Every Christian should strive to be Christlike no matter where they are or what they are doing. The degree and extent of this is uniquely determined, but being a Christian in every sphere of life is not up for debate. From a human responsibility perspective, part of the reason our country is the way it is today is that many Christians are passive regarding political and cultural engagement.

Zero Separation

It is impossible to separate yourself from politics because it is the air we breathe. Economics is similar. A believer could say we should separate religion from economics, but that attitude is just as improbable as separating oneself from politics. Politics is all around us.

- We submit to civil authorities.
- We hear political messages everywhere we go.
- We have opinions on political perspectives, whether we share them or not.
- We're pro-life when it comes to the personhood of a human at conception.
- We pay taxes for virtually everything.
- We watch football players kneel during our national anthem.

It does not matter where you go; politics will always be with you. Each of us must decide whether we will insert our Christian worldview into the conversation according to the ability, time, calling, and influence that the Lord has given us. Or are we going to censor ourselves?

- You engage in politics every day as politicians legislate for or against your Christian beliefs.
- You have an opinion and should share your perspective on how our country should live morally.

If God can use you to slow down the cultural and political

tsunami that has been overrunning us for decades, wouldn't it be wise to speak now? Somewhere between building a theocracy—priests running the government—on Earth and political passivity, millions of Christians should be using God's wisdom to create a better world. The degree and kind will vary, but we cannot pretend we have no role as fellow image-bearers.

Call to Action

1. How could you use your gifts, skills, and talents to make life easier for others from a political perspective? Consider infants in the womb, the elderly, or the freedom to exercise our religion.
2. How much time do you want to allocate to political endeavors? You can vote. What else? What about teaching your children a Christocentric political worldview?
3. What is God calling you to do in the political space? Some Christians choose to be electricians, while others choose a political career. Neither has to be wrong.
4. How much influence do you have persuading others politically? If you're married with children, consider influencing your family first. What about your friends?
5. If you have an opportunity to make your world a better place to live out your Christlike life, wouldn't it be wise to do what you can to accomplish this good outcome?
6. Would it be okay for you to sit passively on the sidelines while politicians create laws that keep you on the sidelines, never able to share the gospel?
7. Is it right for you to keep silent if the government tells you that you cannot teach your children about Jesus?

I trust this book will inspire you as you explore how God may use you to make a difference in the lives within your spheres. Doing life over coffee with a friend and working through the few questions I have asked might be a good start for conversations for transformation.

Introduction

The Bible is clear: those who forget God will not endure (Job 8:13). This truth applies not only to nations but also to churches and individuals. God, who sits enthroned above the Earth, sees all inhabitants as mere grasshoppers (Isaiah 40:22). When a nation turns away from God, it sets in motion a process of escalating chaos, disunity, and eventual destruction. It is tragic and ironic that many of today's leaders—whether in politics or media—fail to recognize this historical pattern. While no nation is without flaws, America's historical success has often paralleled its alignment with Christian principles. However, as we drift from these foundations, the fabric of our society begins to unravel.

Believing the Bible

God's sovereign rulership does not require our acknowledgment or acceptance to make it factual. God's way is right and true regardless of our allegiance to Him and His Word. The call to action for all people and nations is to repent of their sins and trust God (Proverbs 28:`3; Matthew 4:17). We see this necessity demonstrated with Jonah calling the country of Nineveh to repentance (Jonah 3:1-2) and the Lord calling the rich young ruler to faith (Matthew 19:16-22). The calls are the same; we must all bow our knees to the Lord. The decision is ours regarding when we will do it, whether in this life or the one to come. The proactive, humble human sees the wisdom and benefit of following the Lord of the universe today instead of later.

> Therefore God has highly exalted him and bestowed on him the name that is above every name, so that at the name of Jesus every knee should bow, in heaven and on earth and under the earth, and every tongue confess that Jesus Christ is Lord, to the glory of God the Father.
>
> (Philippians 2:9-11)

The integrity of this worldview stands on the legitimacy of God's Word (2 Timothy 3:16-17; John 17:17), which brings us to the most crucial question we can ever ask ourselves. Is the Bible true? Your answer to that pivotal, game-changing question will determine your next question and the trajectory of your life. Faith comes by hearing, and hearing comes by the Word of God, but if anyone disbelieves and discredits God's Word, they will not come to faith in God and never experience the benefits of adoption into His family (Romans 10:9, 13). Our starting point will determine the course of our lives, making the Bible the nonnegotiable starting block to live well in the Lord's world. Do you believe God's Word? See 2 Samuel 7:28; Psalm 19:9, 119:160.

We come to regenerate faith by God imposing Himself in our lives; it's a spiritual decision that is personal and unique to each individual (Romans 10:9, 13). Trusting and following God does not mean we'll have all the answers to the world's problems. We'll never be able to understand all life's complexities, inconsistencies, and disappointments (Isaiah 55:8-9; Psalm 92:5; Amos 4:13; Micah 4:12; 1 Corinthians 2:14). But trusting God regardless of outcomes is your best life now and in eternity.

Competing Worldviews

If a person chooses not to believe in God in a salvific sense—"you must be born again," they must turn to other objects to worship. God implanted in every human a desire to worship, and that desire does not turn itself off if we reject our Creator (Ezekiel 23:7; Leviticus 26:1). We need something outside of ourselves to trust, embrace, obey, and follow. These objects of worship become our agendas, passions, and belief systems. Eventually, these belief systems become so crucial to us and cherished by us that any perceived attack on them is an insult that requires a defense—a counterattack. A Christian will die for his faith, and a non-Christian will harm you if you threaten their faith—the things they cherish the most.

The result is a world with competing belief systems. Without the governing respect for the Imago Dei, these fierce adherents to their anti-Christian belief systems assume they can no longer coexist because if someone does not believe as they believe, they must make life intolerable for them. From this juncture, each worship demographic strategizes how to make their belief system the dominant worldview in the culture or nation. I am not speaking of Christians regarding this point. We believe the Lord provides repentance to all those who want to follow Him, and it's not our responsibility to manipulate or mandate Christian faith on anyone (2 Timothy 2:24-25). The gift of Christianity is a gift that only God can give (Ephesians 2:8-9).

In our country, those who oppose God are winning the cultural scrimmage. They have learned that they can win by legislating their beliefs into the cultural mainstream and by owning the institutions that have the power to gaslight the public. Their strategy is to own the zeitgeist by force or our willful resignation. Their primary modus operandi is to lobby the government to mandate laws to support their belief system. They leverage the governmental political class to persecute those who reject their views. They legally separate our religion from the government while legislating their religious and moral views into our way of life.

Practical Mobilization

Without a revival from the Christian world, the incrementalization of the predominant culture's belief system will eventually become society's dominant thought and practice. Sadly, too many Christians have had a stay-away attitude regarding culture and politics. Their "you leave me alone, and I will leave you alone" mantra is a one-sided affair. The culture is at war with Christianity whether we want to accept it or not. Unwittingly, too many of us have ceded the government's turf to the liberal, progressive activists who took it gladly, and they have no intention of leaving us alone.

The followers of God will have to do more than complain about the societal ills or preach against our country's moral decay, which are the two main reactions when Christians lose conservative cultural ground. We must mobilize practically. The adversary does not care if we preach from our social media platforms into the echo chamber of our "congregations." Preaching to the choir against the woes of a nation becomes a form of public grumbling if there is no practical plan to confront the encroachments of those tearing away at our country's moral fabric.

Of course, others sentimentalize how this country is not their home. This type of spiritualized passivity flies in the face of the Great Commission (Matthew 28:19-20), an active call to action to go and make disciples of the nations. It would behoove the Christian world to rethink how to make disciples. Those on the other side, who despise God and His followers, have a strategic approach to making their disciples. Then some say, "God will win in the end."

That, too, is a form of spiritualized passivity that dismisses our missional calling to convert others to Christ. Yes, God will win in the end. But we must not deny the process that includes our cooperation with God, as secondary causal agents, as we wait for Christ's future rulership to come.

Call to Action

Each Christian must seek God's guidance and learn from one another how to respond to the challenges of our time. While we are not advocating for a theocratic government, we must recognize our God-given responsibility to be salt and light in the world. Our current challenges are generational, and our response must be both practical and deeply rooted in the Great Commission. Now is the time to act, to be the influence that God has called us to be in our respective spheres, and to trust that He will use our efforts for His glory.

1. What will you do?
2. How are you to respond to the cultural demise of your Christian beliefs?
3. In what ways can you practice the Great Commission in your community?
4. How can you emulate those on the other side, in their zeal, without resentment, hostility, fear, hatred, vengeance, or a desire to punish anyone?

1

A Country Analyzed

When it comes to human relationships and societal structures, there are threads of unity and discord woven side by side. It's a delicate balance between building up and tearing down and often hinges on subtle attitudes and actions that can go unnoticed until the fabric frays. I want to explore this delicate balance between unity and discord by discussing how the insidious nature and destructive patterns of autoimmunity, verificationism, and psychosis create a sadistic, triune collective that, if left unchecked, can unravel the very essence of our families, churches, and nations. My goal isn't merely to identify these common traits that can infect all of us but to seek pathways to restoration grounded in the timeless truths that call us to love beyond ourselves.

Befriending the Others

One thing you need to remember as we progress is that everyone you rub shoulders with is not a Christian, and even within our large Christian family, there are many disagreements. Some of your friends come from the other side of the political aisle. You could choose any other metric for comparison, and in all cases, there will not be symmetry in your beliefs or preferences. Our differing worldviews and solutions to problems are something you want to remember as you proceed because seeking unity with those who are not like you is what I will ask you to do in the end.

Furthermore, if you can only be friends with or learn from those you agree with, you are operating at a lower level of Christianity that is bound to bind you into a growthless echo chamber. Suppose you choose to live among the parrots. In that case, you will sabotage your transformative possibilities and interfere with the more significant restoration that could take place in your family, church, or country. God's common grace is on all people. We can learn from those who are different from us and even make peace with a few of them.

Christians hold truth and love in balance, and the wise, humble person knows how to employ this hybrid for the highest good of all, which is God's fame. Sometimes, in our frustration with how "they do things," we end up doing similar things by attacking them. This reactive attitude inevitably tears down the structure or system we say we love, whether it's a family, church, or country. Thus, with a warning in our sightlines, let's move forward with three vital words that speak to this analysis: autoimmune, verificationism, and psychosis. I first heard these words from the liberal scientist Brett Weinstein, though I'm taking a different angle in my use of them.

Autoimmune Disease

Immunity is a healthy body with an immune system that can distinguish between healthy and unhealthy cells. A healthy body attacks the foreign cells, which is the body's way of maintaining unity, wholeness, health, and longevity. Autoimmunity is the opposite of this process. The body does not recognize healthy cells. It is as though these rogue cells are moving through the body wearing a blindfold. They will react to healthy cells, attempting to destroy them. Rather than the body fortifying and defending against evil, it turns on and destroys itself.

We are watching a surreal illustration of a country with an autoimmune disease. It's happening in slow-motion as radical cells attack a good, albeit imperfect, country, thinking they are doing a greater good. In reality, and ironically, they are killing the very thing that gives them the life and freedom to attack and destroy themselves. When your body flips immunity to autoimmunity, you're not far from a debilitating disease leading to inevitable death.

These rogue radicals have been in our body since the inception of our country. Like our physical bodies, we're constantly carrying about those things that can destroy us. Typically, our immune system is robust and healthy enough to withstand the assaults of radicals. In our country's case, there has been a slow and steady building of these radicals in our academic, media, and entertainment indoctrination centers for decades. We are experiencing the full effect of what an autoimmune disease can do to a country.

Autoimmune Applied

However, let's bring it down to a ground-level view. We see a similar thing in the body of Christ—the church. The winds of radical change have always blown through God's church. The Lord has permitted the rise of these radicals, and then a new, invigorated, and trimmed-down church would write a creed to reposition itself against those destructive forces. The strongest wind blowing in our churches today comes from the social Marxist-rooted teaching of Critical Theory, which has given life to such things as social justice.

The social justice problem is not the only issue. Our churches' theological immaturity has sunk to infighting over any imaginable, secondary, preferential matter. Perhaps what I'm saying is oversimplifying the problems for some folks, but in another sense, it's not. When you compare the horrific persecution of the early church and the church in some countries today, a few of us are petty over our precious secondary issues. We have become an autoimmune disease within the body of Christ.

You can diagnose yourself on this matter by assessing how you think and respond to those different from you regarding your [precious preference] or [pick your problem]. If your position is to attack without seeking to discuss it with the individual, you have the early onset of an autoimmune disease. If you want to see what this looks like uncensored, spend twenty minutes on social media reading the Christians' posts. I take that back: only spend ten minutes. If you're not careful, you'll become like our thought leaders. They seem to have lost their moorings on reconciliation and can only attack within their echo chamber of like-minded parrots—also called grandstanding or preaching to the choir.

Verificationism

Verificationism is the process of believing something and verifying your view with any data supporting your settled presupposition. When people want to prove something they already believe, they look for things that affirm their perspective. It's like the preacher with an idea he wants to preach, so he searches for a text to confirm his latest hot take, even if he has to twist the Scripture to make his pet point. In that way, verificationism and eisegesis are similar.

An example of this would be someone who believes that all white people are racist or all police officers are corrupt. If you lock those two presuppositions in your mind, you will always find the data you're looking for to support what you already believe. Verificationism should not be an issue if you look at the data first without a preexisting notion and let the collection of information prove what is right or wrong.

If the text proves his point wrong, the preacher should not preach his message from that passage, choosing to give up on his hot take. Take the perspective that all white people are racists. You look at a broad demographic of white people, examine all the pertinent evidence, and if some of the data proves your thesis is wrong, then you are wrong. The humble soul wants to know the truth, so they let the data determine their belief systems.

Verificationism Applied

You also see verificationism happening in too many marriages and families. It's the frustrated wife who has had enough of her husband's nonsense. Her complaint is valid; he's a jerk, manipulator, [fill in the blank]. At some point, she can only see him as a bad person. She does not begin with an "in the image of God" presupposition. She starts with "his Adamic fallenness." Like the preacher looking for a text to support his thesis, she will always find her husband's flaws.

Some of you may read this and react, "Let me tell you about my husband." If so, you sped too quickly by the part where I said she has a "valid complaint." I would never downsize any legitimate complaint about another fallen person. But if your first instinct is the problem and not the Problem-solver, you have an early onset of autoimmunity; you're attacking the one-flesh union, which is a fallen presupposition. You may come back with, "He's attacking me!" Yes, I understand, but his autoimmunity does not mean you should invite his disease to inhabit your body, a view that we see on both sides of our country's political aisle.

PERSONAL ILLUSTRATION: My mother developed autoimmunity when her daughter-in-law murdered her son, who was my brother. Her objective autoimmunity presupposition turned her into a cynical, bitter, pessimistic, critical person. I'm sharing this story with you to let you know that I understand legitimate hurt. If any problem is greater than God's power to restore our souls, despite what happened to us, then we have autoimmunity and are part of the problem, though we were the victim initially.

Psychosis

The psychotic person is double-minded, which is a better label for the biblically-based, solution-oriented person. There is an element of having two minds or competing belief systems running parallel to each other inside a person's head simultaneously. Having two beliefs at the same time should not be a problem. It's when these two beliefs stop working together for the unifying building up of the person. It's when these two perspectives are forever colliding, asymmetrically stepping on each other, and in a continual battle inside the mind—a psychotic mind.

As you continue interacting with someone with contradictory perspectives aggressively battling each other, you may conclude he is insane. The incompatibilities inside his head are so diverse that he has no clear understanding of himself or what is happening to the world in which he lives. If you bring my psychotic illustration into a contemporary setting, our country has psychosis. We have two competing ways of thinking about virtually everything. These two views are so opposed to each other that there is a growing consensus that our country is becoming insane. The other side looks at us and scratches their heads. We look at them and conclude they are psychotic (crazy). Both sides miss the fact that we are diagnosing ourselves. If they are crazy, then I am, too. We are part of the same body—America. Missing this point could mean the believer loses their biblio-centric anchor point and drifts into la-la land.

Psychosis Applied

If you are part of any unit—marriage, family, church, or country—that you diagnose as crazy, you are diagnosing yourself, too. Suppose you believe only the other person is crazy. In that case, you will find data to support your claim (verificationism), and you will develop an (autoimmune) disease that will permit you to attack the body you are part of (psychosis). That unit—including you—will die soon.

If you believe that you're standing outside of a body you are part of, as though you're not part of it, the psychosis could be so permeated and complicated that you're blind to it. If you're unsure what this looks like in real life, perhaps you can listen to the mostly peaceful protestors of 2020 as they justified their actions, which they believed was a self-prescribed mandate to destroy a country. It was full-on autoimmunity, in plain sight, using the principle of verificationism, that has led to our country's psychosis.

There is hope if you're at the place where you can recognize any of these tendencies in you. If you don't see any of them in you, perhaps a prayer, asking the Lord to open your eyes, would be a rational response. All of us have the potential for the diagnosis I have outlined here. If you believe it and work to change it, then you're part of the solution. We must ask the Lord to provide us with those doors of opportunity for a path forward, whether in our marriages, families, churches, or country.

A Path Forward

The solution is to find someone you can talk to in that group of people on the other side. Rather than attacking them, ask the Father to give you the grace, courage, compassion, and wisdom to see things through their eyes. I'm not suggesting that you must agree with them, though that could be a good thing. I'm suggesting that you seek to understand them, which is the beginning of a humble, civil discourse.

This practice is at the heart of a wise counselor. The counselor may never agree with the person he is helping, but he knows his first obligation to bring restoration is to understand the person sitting on the other side of the room. If he's unwilling to sit, ask, listen, and understand, he will never help—never be part of the solution. To say it differently, you should never "believe all women," but you must understand the woman in front of you if you expect to bring transformative help.

Call to Action

1. What level of autoimmunity do you have? In what specific and practical way do you need to change? Who are you going to talk to about this?
2. What level of verificationism is operating in you? In what specific and practical way do you need to change? Who are you going to talk to about this?
3. What level of psychosis is affecting you? In what specific and practical way do you need to change? Who are you going to talk to about this?
4. Do you already have discourse with those who believe differently from you? I hope so. Let me say it another way: you do know those who are different from you. Think about your doctor, nurse, teacher, auto mechanic, local store clerk, manicurist, church member, and hardware store associate. You have a list of folks with whom you intersect in your day-to-day life. This idea of reaching across the aisle, fence, living room, or yard is not a foreign concept to any of us.
5. What do you need to do to change yourself so that you can interact with those who believe and act differently from you?

2

A New Slave Owner

Our country is in a tailspin. The most popular word an immediate pathway to cancellation in America today is racism. Two hundred-plus years of striving and tension around race are spilling over into our streets and onto our social media platforms. The noise is so loud. It's annoying, tedious, concerning, and a lie. Some people are reacting with no filter, while others want to bury their self-censoring heads in the sand. Why are we here? What happened to us? More importantly, what can we do?

Sin and Idealism

Idealism is at the core of the racism problems we face today. Competing groups have their non-nuanced views on their truth regarding racism (John 14:6). Because sin penetrates and complicates all idealistic perspectives, anyone's best plans and aspirations can take radical turns to keep them from their ideals while deforming their good intentions into something more insidious (Romans 5:12). The civil rights movement, for example, was born out of the ideal that America is a great country. Martin Luther King often talked about the guiding principles of this country, which gave him confidence that we would win the fight against racism.

He believed that America was great and could reach higher because the Declaration of Independence laid out a roadmap for the equality of all people. Even though many of the framers of America's plan for our future had slaves, they inherently knew that it was not right and that our country could do better. Like the addict who knows what he's doing is wrong and understands there is a better way, the stain of sin flowed from the framer's pens as they wrote about an ideal future (Romans 7:21-25). A flawed penman does not necessarily invalidate his writings, or nobody could put a quill to parchment.

Sinner and Saint

Mercifully, their desire for what was moral motivated them to press on with their notion that all men and women are created equal and should have the same rights in this land of the free (James 4:17). America could have stayed a country that promoted slaves, but our forefathers, though guilty of the sins they were writing against, did not capitulate from the ideal of moving America forward. They penned the documents that caused a country to take a moral leap from a dark past, hoping that progress, idealism, courage, and change would be in our future. King, a fellow sinner/saint, understood our mutual sinner/ saint complex, which is why he did not separate himself from the framers of our country, as though he were more innocent, but inserted himself into the continuum they had started.

We, too, are ever-evolving (1 John 1:9). We were not what we should have been. Still, we strove for a better version of ourselves (1 Peter 2:2). To expect perfection of our old selves is as illogical as a parent demanding the perfect one-year-old, two-year-old, or three-year-old (Ephesians 4:22-24). Common sense and the logical realities of human fallenness must level the ground upon which we all stand, or we might think we are brighter than those who went before us because we use lamps not candles. America, in its infant state, was not perfect, and history has never tried to hide our blemishes. The stain of the fall was all over our country then, as it is now. We can be honest about our pasts while always trying to improve from what we used to be (Colossians 3:9).

The New Activist

King could not have anticipated how those who came after him would not follow the 200-year continuum that was bringing change. He believed in the American dream, which said it did not matter what the color of your skin was but the content of your character (Romans 5:3-5). He taught that becoming educated, working hard, and providing for your family were three vital ingredients to personal freedom and advancement (1 Timothy 5:8). He intuitively knew that personal responsibility was a vital key to unlocking the door to America's privileges. Regrettably, the new activist chose another route to a different kind of freedom, a freedom that does not set the captive free (Colossians 3:5). Education, hard work, and the family were not instantly gratifying enough for the new reformers.

They demanded that governmental engineers do the heavy lifting. Unwittingly, the modern activists rejected the traditional slave owner for a new one. Rather than seeing the grace and the guilt of Thomas Jefferson and his friends, they only saw the error of the framers' ways. Their inability to recognize the reality of the stain of sin on all things, they drew a circle around the past, labeled it anathema, and tossed it into the trash heap that is on the wrong side of history. Rather than following King on the continuum to newer, unfolding freedoms, they embraced a darkened attitude (Psalm 75:4), saying,

It's all wrong. We're going to force the government to socially engineer what we want. If the government does not give us what we want, we will tear down America.

They are yet to realize how their chucking of the past and embracing a new slave mentality will take them back into the slavery that they disdain.

Conflating Equality and Disparity

The irony is appalling as you watch so many Americans, black and white, marching toward the slave blocks of the government. The new activists are bowing to a different paternalistic master. The potent fuel that feeds their anger is race envy. The new activist sees a disparity between individuals and demographics. They mandate that racial, economic, and social equality must come to everyone now. It's the newly married couple who demands that they have all the perks and pleasures of their parents without doing the work that brought those things to their parents. The American way holds out opportunities for anyone. Some people will have more obstacles, but there is plenty of anecdotal evidence to suggest that if you want it and are willing to work for it, the chances of obtaining your dream are higher in this country than in any other.

America has done a better job reforming itself than any other country in the world. The confusion comes when folks conflate equality and disparity. Jefferson, King, and others pushed for every American to have an equal chance, but that does not mean the results will be identical. When you take a wide-angle view of how America has changed, it's stunning. We've never been so close to equality for all, but if you believe that equality should lead to the same results for everyone, you will never be happy and always be angry.

Enter White Guilt

After the activists stamped and rejected the past as evil, and the only way to make it right was through manipulated governmental intervention, America began its descent to where we are today. It's a great regression. It's that newly married couple who believes that disparity is a wicked inequality, and the only way to fix it is for someone outside of themselves to give them stuff they did not earn so they have as much as their parents. The idealism of Martin Luther King, who believed America had come a long way, baby, but was not quite there yet, changed to we're going to get there today through governmental engineering. Their logic says,

> We are walking away from the hard-fought freedom of our forefathers, who were black and white, and rather than continue the fight for freedom their way, which is foundational to what it means to be an American, we're going to embrace an entitlement attitude.

One of the strongest weapons of choice for the post-King activist is white guilt. There is truth in the word guilt because many who went before us were profoundly guilty of horrendous acts of racial violence against black Americans. No rational person would deny these realities. Saying that some white people are guilty is accurate, but to label every white person in America—past and present—as guilty is an overreach that will incarcerate or destroy both whites and blacks.

The Postmodern Slave

With redrawn battle lines, it was no longer a fight for freedom through hard work, educational advancement, and strengthening the black family. The new activists placed their hopes in manipulating white people into contrition, hoping this gaslit guilty demographic would do their bidding through their governmental privilege and autocratic mandates. The new activists mixed real guilt with gaslit white guilt, which produced their sense of entitlement. The evolving freedoms that Martin Luther King led a generation to shifted toward a fixation on the slave master government to bring about equality for all through whatever means necessary. King distanced the black community from slavery, which depended on the conjured benevolence of their masters. The new activists moved the cause away from America's moral progress by swerving toward the government as the new master that would bring the long-awaited equality for all.

The old-time slave was dependent on his master. The post-modern slave is hitching his shackles to the lustful government. The new slaves make their appeals to the predominantly white, paternalistic political elite to give them a handout. The detrimental irony of this handshake with the devil is that the modern slave owner does not genuinely love the black person. The white liberal uses the black person to assuage their self-imposed white guilt while keeping the black community in bondage to their enticing programs, which keeps the master in charge and the black person enslaved.

The New Liberal Ecosystem

This bargain with the devil and facade of love has its appeal, especially when the handouts come. It's sad to watch each politically liberal-minded person fall all over themselves to give more stuff than the last liberal-minded elite. Its liberal one-upmanship as the faux-sympathetic paternal slave master proves their sorrow over the past by giving out more to those who believe they are entitled. The black person who bows to their governmental masters believes it's an advancement in privilege. It's not. It's a lie. It's re-enslaving. The master is catching the slave all over again. In blindness, the black person applauds the manipulative paternal government for giving them what they wanted.

The white person experiences vindication for their white guilt, and the black person senses equality. Meanwhile, the black person continues to be small in this reimagined, liberal ecosystem, but there is more irony: the entitled blacks and paternal liberals blame the conservatives for where we are. It's incredible how liberalism gave us the KKK, abortion, and other oppressive groups and initiatives, and it was the conservatives who fought along with the blacks for their freedom. This new pact with the devil is complete: The entitled black looks to the predominately paternalistic white politician. Both groups blame conservatives for how messed up our country is today.

What Liberals Need

The surreal truth in this political power play is that conservatives don't want to rule over blacks. We don't see them as inferior or unequal. We see them like us: all of us are Americans. We believe in cooperating with others to help everyone gain all their aspirations. Conservatives embrace equal freedom for everyone, which puts destiny in the hands of the responsible to become whatever they desire. From George Washington to Martin Luther King, our country was making tremendous progress. Despite our sins, moral advancement was happening. Of course, this created a problem for the liberal power brokers. The only way they can survive is to make promises, give away free stuff, and create a dependent class. If equality did come, there would be no place for the liberal, power-hungry political elite. They need our country to swerve off the path of steady transformation. If freedom did ring, they would be out of business. They had to change things, which they did in eleven sequential steps.

1. The liberal gave a fake admittance of their white guilt about white privilege.
2. They mapped their faux-confession over every white person, past and present.
3. The emboldened black person accepted their apology.
4. The black person demanded penance in return (entitlement).
5. The white liberal agreed and promised the moon— one moon at a time.
6. The duped black person shook on it, which was a step back into bondage.
7. The liberals felt exonerated for their past sins.
8. The black person is grateful for the handout.
9. The liberal is still the master.
10. The black person is the slave.
11. The disparity between whites and blacks widens.

Call to Action

Racial problems are complicated, and they won't change anytime soon. Though there will never be perfect harmony in a sin-cursed world, we can get back to making progress. My appeal to you is to think less globally about the problem and more personally. It's easy to be swept away by the problems you see in the media. It's wiser to step away from their noise and focus on what you can change. Try this instead.

1. Examine your heart for any hate toward any person—black, white, friend, family member, spouse, parent, church leader, etc.
2. Who do you dislike? Is there a person with whom you harbor any animosity? If so, who is that person? What do you need to do to change?
3. Ensure you understand the problem of racial tension in our culture. Don't succumb to or spend time listening to the media outlets that teach a different narrative. Feed your mind with truth, God's truth.
4. Talk to your friends about these matters. Convince one person at a time. If you have a larger platform, use it for God's fame, helping any person that you can.
5. Keep in mind that our most significant hope is in Christ alone. Don't become hung up on where our country is; focus on what you believe and who you can influence. I'm speaking of the Great Commission: go and make disciples.
6. Guard your heart against the gaslighting of the liberal voices. You will become and cooperate with what you feed your mind. Fill your mind with God's Word and its appropriate applications.
7. The truth will win out; it always does. Corrupt people will continue to overreach to their demise.

8. Recommended Resource: Shelby Steele's book, *"Shame: How America's Past Sins Have Polarized Our Country,"* from which I gleaned many of these thoughts.

3

Woke Degrees

One of the most hotly debated terms this century is the word woke. It means to be aware, as in, "I have woke up to [this cause]." Formerly, you were not aware; now, you are. Woke is most often used in the context of what some folks believe are the oppressors and the oppressed: "I am awake to your oppression of me." Within this group of woke people, you will find a spectrum of adherents. On one end, there are the innocent idealists, and on the other, there are angry activists.

Woke Origins

It is theologically fair to say the first woke people were Adam and Eve. They were doing pretty well in the Garden of Eden before the walking, talking, oppressive serpent opened their eyes to another way of thinking about God, life, each other, and social causes. In Genesis 3:6, Adam and Eve became woke. The idea of woke has been around for several millennia and used in different ways. It appears that the modern expression of woke entered common speech in 2008 in the black community.

In today's culture, wokeness has glommed onto itself a specific and intensified meaning. You can be woke about many things, though most of the time, people connect their wokeness to the social justice movement. More on that later. To trace wokeness to its modern origins, you would go back to the Frankfurt School in the 1930s, where you'll learn about Critical Theory (CT)—the roots of woke, and many other synonymous social ideas and constructs.

Frankfurt School

The Frankfurt School was a collection of smart misfits who did not adhere to capitalism or communism's unbending framework. This group of intellectuals believed there was a better way to think about social advancement. They did this by tying themselves to Marxism, not so much with Karl Marx's economic ideas but a Marxist sociological worldview. To be woke, in today's use of the word, means your presuppositional starting point begins in a social Marxist ideology.

Most woke people don't know their woke history, which is one reason many Christians are jumping on the woke wagon. This disconnect in understanding is why woke gainsayers need to understand that all woke people are not created equally. In the context of this chapter, I have on one end of the woke spectrum, the innocent idealists. On the other end is the scold mob, whom I call the angry activists. If you asked the innocent idealist about the presuppositional roots of wokeness, they could not tell you. Someone gave them a sign on a stick and said, "Go stand [over there]." They have never heard of the Frankfurt School, Critical Theory, or Karl Marx.

Roots Matter

What they need to understand is that if they begin with a presuppositional Marxist philosophy on social issues, their activism will be consistent with Karl Marx. The result will be something different from the Bible's endpoint. Most culturally woke people—I assume—do not understand how presuppositions determine their activism and the linear results that flow from that starting point. Because of this lack of awareness, Christians need to respond with humility and intelligence to the innocently unaware. Imagine someone yelling at you about your ignorance before God woke you up to your lostness (Ephesians 2:1-5).

Condemnation strategies may work for a few but not the entire unregenerate or woke communities. Think about how you came to Christ. You were born in Adam, totally depraved, a dirty, rotten sinner, with no hope of ever understanding or changing (1 Corinthians 2:14; John 3:7; Romans 3:10-12, 10:9, 13). From that presuppositional starting point, you grew up as an unregenerate child, acting out according to your Adamic nature. The results would have been hell if you had not become woken in Christ (Revelation 20:15).

A Tree with Branches

The presuppositional root of the woke tree starts with the communist Karl Marx, who gives us critical theory (CT) about social issues. From there, the CT tree grows into many branches. Some of these limbs intersect with each other, while others do not. To borrow another metaphor, think of Critical Theory as a bowl of soup, and inside the container are many social constructs. Here are a few.

- **CRITICAL RACE THEORY (CRT):** The idea that laws, institutions, and structures are systemically racist and must change fundamentally.
- **INTERSECTIONALITY:** The study that any aspect of a person's identity—e.g., race, gender, class—can be an advantage or disadvantage. A black, gay female is part of three disadvantaged groups, according to the theory. She's not as privileged as a white, gay female.
- **WOKENESS:** The person who opens their eyes to see societal ills through the lens of Critical Theory.
- **QUEER THEORY:** A strand of Critical Theory that

teaches a person how to think about or practice being gay.

- **IDENTITY POLITICS:** Believing your identity is the primary way you should think of yourself, e.g., black, LGBTQ+, trans, female, etc.
- **SOCIAL JUSTICE:** Bringing social equality to all vulnerable, weaker, smaller, or less powerful groups.
- **WHITE PRIVILEGE:** Opportunities that white people have and that minorities—people of color (POC)—do not.
- **HEGEMONIC POWER:** The dominance of the more influential group exerting power and authority over the less dominant. This group is the oppressor class.

There are many more Critical Theory constructs, but you get the idea. Those who have given more time to this will provide more comprehensive definitions for all of these concepts, but I hope this abbreviated list provides you with a basic thumbnail sketch and a path forward to think about and care for the woke soul.

The Big Idea

The running theme through all of these constructs is two people groups—the oppressors and the oppressed. If you go back through the shortlist of Critical Theory constructs, you will see how these two antithetical groups conflict. For example, our current cultural crisis is racism. According to the accusation, the whites are the ruling hegemonic power (oppressors), and the blacks are the oppressed. Slavery is the proof in the pudding, according to those who beat the Critical Theory drum. No rational person denies the atrocities of slavery, though that time in our dark history is not as black and white as some folks want to make it today.

There is complexity with slavery in America, but if your

motivation is not as objective as it should be, you will not entertain those complexities. You will stay stuck in a cycle of victimness and hate. The mind-boggling good news is that we abolished slavery and have been progressively removing those evil barriers that kept men and women from a fair shot at the American dream. Because our founding fathers believed in the teachings of Scripture, even though many of them were not Christians, they framed our country with the best possibilities for success. Anyone who takes an honest look at our country's 250-year trend will see this ever-progressing miracle.

Innocent Idealists

But we have flaws. If you put 350+ million sinners in a room, bad things will happen. Like the parent who cannot see a child's positive progression, too many woke people highlight only our negative traits, even if it means tearing down the structures that provided the framework that gives them the freedom and platform to demolish our country. We see the disintegrating of the structures in every corner of our society, including the church.

There are hordes of social justice warriors lashing out within our churches, seeking to bring correction (or tear down) the system. It is no accident that these justice seekers run contemporary with what is happening in the culture. They are not wrong in the sense that we have problems in our house. Abuses are everywhere. I am as attuned to abusive people, churches, and denominations as anyone. I have not disregarded or miscommunicated these things, but it has never occurred to me to remake the body of Christ or its manifestations—local churches.

Sloganeering Bait

The fingerprints of Satan are all over these justice movements, whether inside or outside the church. There is a reason the Bible talks about the devil as an angel of light (2 Corinthians 11:14). I am not saying that these innocent idealists are satanic or even unregenerate. What person has not been duped by the devil? The devil's plan has not changed since he woke up Adam and Eve, and he will not leave us alone either. We all have our guilt, so there's no need to duck: I'm not tossing stones at anyone. Part of his angel of light strategy is in his sloganeering. There is always just enough embedded truth in the Critical Theory mantras to allure any of us.

Who believes that black lives do not matter? No rational person. How clever to say, "Black Lives Matter," but when you look under the hood of that organization, you see a Marxist group who explicitly states their hope to destroy the nuclear family. Or, how can you argue against social justice? Shouldn't all Christians strive to treat all people in all social constructs with fairness? The problem is that these social justice warriors inside the church, whether innocent or not, are tearing down the historical church structure and installing a worldview that has its roots in Karl Marx, the Frankfurt School, and Critical Theory.

Angry Activists

As you move across the spectrum of proponents of the Critical Theory, you will eventually run into the most hostile of these adherents. They are angry, vindictive, anti-God, and would feel no sympathy if a white person were to become a casualty of this culture war. I will not illustrate their hate speech here, but if you're interested, you may jump on nearly any social platform to hear the cliches and vitriol. These warriors are not unaware Marxists. They want to destroy America and any other person or country that believes differently from them. They are the angry cancel culture on steroids. As the non-peaceful protests of 2020 demonstrated, they are not hiding the ball. They want to destroy any person or group that can exert power over them, e.g., police, white people, men, etc.

They won't acknowledge how it's only a minority within all of these groups who are abusive. For example, Robin DiAngelo teaches all white people are guilty of racism in her wildly popular book, *White Fragility*. According to her, if you admit you are a racist, you're guilty—whether your admission was genuine or you caved to gaslighting. If you deny that you're a racist, you prove your guilt by your denial. It is a non-falsifiable circularity, along the lines of the Salem Witch Trials: throw a witch in a pond; if she drowns, she is not a witch; if she walks on water, she is a witch, so they burn her at the stake. Either way, she dies.

Don't Be a Denier

The innocent idealists will do similarly to the angry activists, though they will accomplish their goals with less vitriol. Those who adhere, ignorantly or not, to Critical Theory do so because they believe in their version of utopia, a word that means no place; it does not exist. It would be great if our marriages, churches, workplaces, and culture were better than they are now, but we know that the Bible narrative teaches a sinful world that Christ came to redeem. If you look at the lives of authentic Christians, you will see this progressive transformation. What you won't see is perfection.

For us imperfect Christians who do believe and follow the Bible, we cannot deny that there is some truth in what the CT activists are saying. What you don't want to do is make the mistake of saying "all social justice warriors are evil" by clumping every social justice adherent into the same camp. It's sophomoric to think in such terms. My appeal here is to encourage you to keep influencing, but do it the right way. Ask the Lord to give you the courage to stand on your platform, no matter its size. Too many Christians are afraid to speak out; they want to be left alone, but we do not have that option. We have a light and some salt in our knapsacks. Jesus appeals to us to use those redemptive tools for God's glory and the benefit of as many who will hear, submit, and follow.

Call to Action

Will you do four things in response to this chapter?

1. Study Critical Theory and its constructs.
2. Continue to examine yourself, but not in an overly introspective, navel-gazing way. Ask God to give you appropriate biblical clarity about where you are with these matters.
3. As you are educating yourself and examining your soul, talk to those within your peer group. You will have to guide some of them. Others will be able to have mature, reciprocal conversations with you.
4. Ask the Lord to give you the humility, wisdom, compassion, and courage to influence those who could use your help.

4

The Mask

In 2020, the number one question circulating in people's minds was, "Should I wear a mask?" Perhaps you wore one, and it was a non-issue. Praise God. I'm sure you were aware that many of your friends were not where you were. It never occurred to me to write on this subject, but it proved to be a paper-thin problem that turned into a mountainous stumbling block for too many people. As most of our dilemmas go, we usually begin by asking the wrong question, which makes our mask problem an excellent case study to help us think rightly about the next cultural and political overreach.

Prior Grumbling

Isn't it instructive to think about our grumbling prior to the pandemic? So many of the things we complained about then would be welcomed annoyances today. The universal divisiveness in our culture was at an all-time high, at least in my lifetime. Things have been worse, of course (e.g., the American Revolution and Civil War). Still, I have not experienced life as challenging as it has been lately—from a cultural and political perspective. As I reshuffle the "events of my life hierarchy" with the worst at the top, what is happening today is ascending while my former complaints are moving down a notch or two.

It won't be long before our most common mantra about

the "good old days" will be prior to the 2020 pandemic. Reflecting on how good you had it may teach you how things can worsen—a call to be thankful today for what you have. I'm not sure what to think about how bad it is today when one of the biggest flies in our cultural ointment was about whether we should wear a mask. I suppose folks who live in third-world countries shook their heads at our mask problem. I'm not saying it was not an issue, but what if you reframed it from another perspective?

The Starting Place

For those of you who have been counseling for a while, you know that rarely is the first question a counselee asks is the most vital one they should ask. Typically, a counselee will begin with the external problem, i.e., "my wife won't talk to me," which is what the husband experiences most acutely. They will ask for tips on how to communicate well with each other without biting and devouring one another (Galatians 5:15). Best practices and guidelines on how to communicate well are vital. The counselor will serve them well by providing a few ways they can think about talking without being harsh, judgmental, or silent.

As you help with the practical side of their talk trouble, you want to dig deeper to show them some of the hidden complexities and relational dynamics below the surface. Our mask problem was similar; it was not the most controlling issue. The opening paragraph of the Proverbs of Solomon ends with a statement that gives us guidance on the deeper matters of the heart. Solomon implies that we must have the right starting place before we begin problem-solving. That old verse is the best one for our times. We need knowledge, wisdom, and instruction, but that is not where we want to begin. Do you see the right starting place in this verse?

The fear of the LORD is the beginning of knowledge;
fools despise wisdom and instruction.

(Proverbs 1:7)

A Little Background

I'll get back to Solomon in a moment, but first, may I make an appeal? As you proceed with any secondary matter, the most challenging thing for any of us is to be slow to speak and quick to listen (James 1:19). Will you bear with me? I realize that many people get bent-out-shape about things like masks. I understand the tension. The left side of our political spectrum has pushed their agendas farther than they have ever gone before, and it's bugging some of us while tempting others to fear in ways that are debilitating. When you look at today's evolving political spectrum, you see everything sliding leftward.

There used to be the liberal left with whom most of the conservatives did battle. Those folks continue to exist, but there is another group on the other side of them that makes liberals look conservative. It's not like these socialists, communists, and Marxists have not been around. They have always been here. The difference is that there was a time when the left and right had one immutable dividing line of agreement that said America is a great country, though we differed on which worldview should be preeminent to make us better.

Fear and Frustration

Many people believe that an invisible force is pulling liberals and conservatives into a dark, left-leaning black hole. Their fear or frustration intensifies as they watch the shifting of the Overton Window. At the top of the window are the more radical ideas of the culture. The farther you go to the bottom, the more conservative you become. The problem is the continual upward momentum of the Overton Window.

It's changing what acceptable talking points are. For example, being gay used to be outside the Overton Window of acceptable behavior. Today, being gay is near the center of the window, while disagreeing with gayness has fallen through the bottom.

You're a homophobe if you believe being gay is wrong. As the Overton Window continues to move upward, our culture will embrace more ideas that used to be taboo, while historical, conservative views will fall from the bottom of the window, making those formerly acceptable ideas phobic and worthy of our cancellation, or even worse. As the Christian community sees the slow eroding of their beliefs, their fear and frustration levels rise higher than their faith in what God might do with our skirmishes.

A Better Question

- How do you follow along when you believe someone is pulling you into a world that you disdain?
- Should you give up this ground or stand fast?
- What if you give up a little for now and return later after things settle down?
- Will things settle or continue to change forever?

These questions—plus a few others—explain the problem with our masks, which is why you must be careful when addressing what should be an easy question to answer. It's not. The mask is a metaphor for a world gone mad. Should you wear a mask? The world was divided over this minor question, and so was the church. On a more granular level, friends and families felt the pinch, too. To add to the complexity, many folks in the culture were watching us. A few of them laughed, mocked, and jeered, while others felt affirmation because they always cynically knew that Christianity is full of fake and immature Christians.

This angst brings us back to Solomon. Solomon wants us to go back to the beginning of knowledge to make sure that we're at the right spot before we answer the question about wearing a mask. He wants us to calibrate our hearts. If you don't do this, you won't think rightly about masks or anything else. Where is this right spot? Solomon places the starting place for all knowledge in the fear of God.

The Fear of God

The fear of the Lord is the beginning of knowledge. If you want to know what to do about wearing a mask, you must address your understanding of the fear of God. Do you know what that term means? If so, how is the fear of God actively monitoring and guiding you as you think about the "should I wear a mask" quandary? The fear of God has two parts: God is a God of judgment and a God of love, both of which you see at the dawn of humanity. After Adam and Eve sinned, there was a judgment on them, but God was not just the punisher of sin: He provided a sacrifice for them so that they would not have to pay for their transgressions.

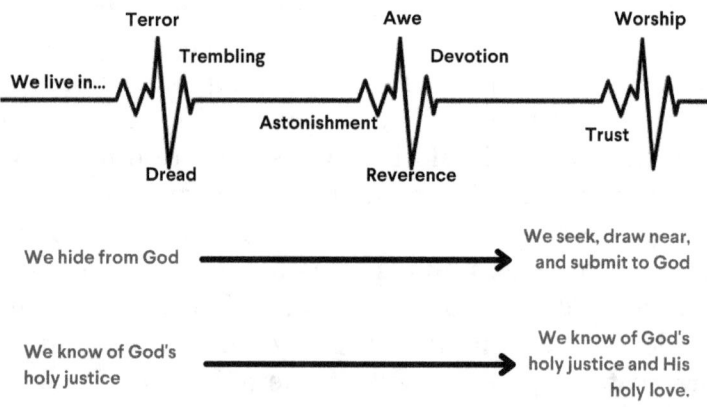

Fear of Man - Fear of God Continuum

(c) Ed Welch - Used By Permission

- A God of wrath and judgment only leads to an unhealthy and self-damaging view of the Lord.
- A God of love only gives you a toothless Santa that takes you down a path of any self-conceived luxury or lust.

The balanced Christian has a healthy fear of God, an awe-filled fear that rests in His astonishing love because the believer knows that Christ forever judged their most significant problem in life. This Christian is not just restful; their peace shapes how they think about God, self, others, and life. The fear of God is why a mask does not manage them.

Test Your Response

If you lean one way or another on the fear of the Lord spectrum, your attitude and responses to others will reflect it. For example, if you are overly harsh, stubborn, critical, unkind, resentful, and frustrated about this mask thing, you're not at peace, and you will lean toward the judgment side of things. Judgment people tend to be harsher with how they think about matters of practice.

If you're more afraid, manipulatable, willing to go with the flow, and characterized by anxiousness when thinking about the mask thing, you're leaning too much toward the love side of things. Love must have courage, or it's not love at all. This person is afraid to take a stand, also called the fear of others (Proverbs 29:25). Their compromised love becomes a failed attempt to keep others from being unkind to them. If your love does not have a backbone, don't call it love because it's not. You're fearful.

- The judgment-leaning person is stubborn, harsh, and angry.
- The love-leaning person is weak, afraid, and managed.

A person who understands the fear of God is in the right place to have the right knowledge. They are not unkind toward others or afraid to take a stand. Because the fear of the Lord manages them, they can think rightly about all things regarding life and godliness, including our cultural mask problem.

What Do You Believe?

I could provide you with a long list of things that I believe and do, and some of you would be offended. These things are not sinful to me, but some folks would not agree because a few of those preferential practices grind against their souls. Because of this tension, if I know that [fill in the blank] bothers you, I will not do it in front of you (James 4:17). It would be unkind to do so. Of course, the comeback is, "But what if it's not a sin? Are you to bow to every whim, preference, peculiarity, and quirk of someone?" The answer is obvious if you understand and practice the fear of the Lord.

- If you bow to every preference that someone has, you are love-leaning with little courage.
- If you blow off someone because they are immature and need to get over themselves, you are judgment-leaning without kindness.

Neither instance is the wisdom of Solomon. If you fall one way or the other, you need to get alone with God and work out your skewed understanding and practice of the fear of the Lord. It would be wise and helpful to connect with someone more mature than you are to repair your fear of God problem. As you correct it, you will grow in wisdom, which is how you're going to figure out how to answer the mask question. I suspect some folks will read these ideas, expecting me to answer the mask question for them. These folks lack understanding and tend to want others to solve their problems without them doing the hard work of wrestling with God. Ninety-nine percent of all your questions are not in the Bible—in an explicit way.

Will You Do This?

You have to make your decision about wearing a mask— or the next thing—based on where you are with the Lord. Specifically, it will be your understanding and practice of the fear of God. If you're too harsh or too manipulated by others, you're not at the right starting point, and you will not make the best decision or react properly to others. If you are frustrated or fearful, the essential thing you should do is ask someone about your attitude, words, and actions regarding the secondary controversial preference of the moment.

If a Christian is unwilling to do that, then they are not a humble person, and you have your answer about where they are with the Lord. If they persist, they will stir up strife (James 4:6). But if the humble believer is willing to solicit input from one or two competent, compassionate, and courageous friends, they will be able to adjust themselves biblically. The kind of friend you're looking for to assist you in the biblically informed decision-making process has these core components of friendship:

- **COMPETENT:** They are skilled in God's Word.
- **COMPASSIONATE:** They demonstrate kindness toward others.
- **COURAGEOUS:** They are not afraid to speak the truth in love.

Talk to them. Make sure you're at the right starting place, which is a proper fear of God, which influences your thoughts and practice. Then, your response to the mask—or the next thing—will be as right as it can be.

Call to Action

The best passage to study mask-wearing is 1 Corinthians 8, where we find one group afraid to eat previously sacrificed meat and another group puffed up about the fearful group.

1. What is your attitude about the controversial preference of the moment? Will you share these things with a friend to get their input? Are you too harsh and unkind or too fearful and lacking courage?
2. What is the most biblical way that you can serve those in your church when it comes to secondary matters that are controversial?
3. What does submission to your church leadership look like for this matter? Are you correct in your response to them? How do you know?
4. How does the ever-moving Overton Window influence your thoughts and responses to the changing times?
5. If you're interacting with someone who is sinfully angry or overly anxious about secondary issues, you could admonish the angry person and encourage the fearful.

5

Racial Irony

There is a twist of irony when one person condemns another, even if the accusation is correct. Jesus was right when He said, "Judge not, that you be not judged. For with the judgment you pronounce you will be judged, and with the measure you use it will be measured to you" (Matthew 7:1-2). To paraphrase, He said that if you choose to dish it out, it will likely come back on you. If we do not guard our hearts when we critique others, we may forget that we are not guilt-free, probably doing adjacent things as we critique those around us. We see this play out a zillion times a day in our country.

Condemning the Condemned

Let me illustrate: do you remember Donald Sterling? He owned an NBA team. There was a media storm over some racist remarks he allegedly made—remarks recorded and turned over to TMZ and then to the public. He lost his basketball team because he's an alleged racist. During that firestorm, Mark Cuban, the owner of the NBA's Dallas Mavericks, weighed in on racism by saying we all are racists in some form or fashion. He went on to stereotype black people with hoodies and white people with tattoos.

His comments set off another storm as the ESPN talking heads pushed his interview to the top of several of their shows, most of them condemning him for acknowledging the universality of racism. The ironic reality of ESPN's perspectives was the prejudice they had toward prejudiced folks. Read that sentence again, slowly. It is a puzzle they do not seem to perceive, presumably because their discrimination is morally superior, at least in their minds, to Mark's. Enter Clay Travis—another sport's talking head—into the fray, who wrote a remarkable follow-up to Cuban and the ESPN talking heads.

> Let's be honest, white people don't write or talk publicly about race unless it's to condemn people for being racist. It's easier that way. The company line from most white people is this: racism is bad and we're not racist. In fact, most white people today fear being called racist more than just about anything in the world. How much so? Put it this way, if your average white person had to choose between getting arrested for a DUI or being publicly branded a racist, just about every single one of us would pick getting a DUI. That's right, we'd rather put countless lives in danger, go to jail and face criminal charges than be called a racist in America today.
>
> – Clay Travis

All Have Sinned

Clay's insight is striking. In a small way, I am a public figure, and what Travis said is not news to me. I have felt the impact of the power brokers with more clout and swagger than I possess in the arena where I play. There are high-powered people in every field, including Christianity. If you speak out against their preferences, people, or politics, they might persuade others to turn against you. I am not for any racist comments from anyone; that is not my point. Racism is wrong—a position all Christians believe. The point here is that there is a "little bit of racism in all of us." The real issue is whether we will be humble and courageous enough to admit it. Travis explained it this way:

> It's 100 percent true. Every single person of every race and ethnicity judges people all day long based on how they look, how they walk, their mannerisms, what they say or do on social media. We all do it. If you doubt me, go read the comments on Instagram or Twitter. Break down what's being said to its root essence, and the vast majority of the time, it's a value judgment of one sort or another—we're all tribal, seeking to classify people as either with us or against us. It's impossible to avoid judging people; we're biologically wired to do so. But we're also smart enough to be conscious of our thoughts and examine whether they're legitimate.
>
> – Clay Travis

Class Prejudice?

> Not that we dare to classify or compare ourselves with some of those who are commending themselves. But when they measure themselves by one another and compare themselves with one another, they are without understanding.
>
> (2 Corinthians 10:12)

Clay is talking about class prejudice. That problem is one of our universal sins, too. We tend to look down on certain kinds of people, irrespective of their skin color. Even if we are not racists, we struggle with class envy or class disdain. *This American Life* aired a podcast called *Americans in Paris*. The last act of their show was about a black American—Janet McDonald—who moved to Paris and stayed partly because French folks didn't treat her the way Americans treated her when she lived in the States. To her surprise, after acclimating to the Parisian way of life, she learned there was another kind of prejudice that was not black but class. She talked to Cornell West about this and shared what he had said to her on the podcast.

> Basically, he suggested it was a class thing. And he said, "Well, you know, look at you, you are professionally articulate. If you brought fifteen of your cousins [to Paris from Brooklyn], it would be a whole different thing." So, basically, he was saying if I brought all my homegirls from the hood, like, who didn't go to Vassar and weren't lawyers and who didn't speak French, you know, the reception might be a little chillier, even though they also are black Americans. I think if that is true, then it is not about racism, but it is about class.
>
> – Janet McDonald

What Kind Are You?

> The Pharisee, standing by himself, prayed thus: "God, I thank you that I am not like other men, extortioners, unjust, adulterers, or even like this tax collector. I fast twice a week; I give tithes of all that I get."
>
> (Luke 18:11-12)

Which are you? Are you a racist or a classist? Or both? Do you divvy people by skin color, or are there particular types of individuals, behaviors, and attitudes you look down on and separate from them regardless of the color of their skin? Maybe it is the guy standing on the street corner with a sign asking for food. Perhaps it is an obese woman with five children delaying you in Walmart because she cannot find all of her food stamps—the ones you paid the government for so that she could stand in line and hinder you. What kind of person stirs your self-righteous heart? I am not judging you. I ask what should be an obvious question because we all have someone we look down on from our high chairs.

Would you say the doctrine of sin has not touched you this way? Have you successfully overcome what the Lord did when He separated people and created languages in Genesis 11:7-8? Mark Cuban is right: we all classify people. The question should not be whether we discriminate but whether we can talk about how we do it. This problem is not something outside the Christian experience, as though we are a better demographic. It is a significant issue within the church, a two-headed dilemma where Sterling's alleged sin and Cuban's honesty highlight connects to us, too. On one side, we want to stand up and speak out against one man's racism, while on the other hand, we should have enough self-awareness to know and humility to admit that we are not all that different from the bigot.

Will We Be Honest?

If your first recourse is to punish someone for being honest, you will send them underground, where the truth about their thoughts and struggles will never see the light of day. It is not wise to complicate a person's sin by disliking them mean-spiritedly. Speaking against a person has its place, but sinfully reacting to them makes us accessories to the future harm they do to themselves or others. The church and ESPN can be similar in this way: we can be quick to condemn a person for being a sinner.

Though I expect this from sports media, Christians can do better because we have the solution for humanity's sinfulness. I have counseled scores of people who were part of religious systems and institutions that punished them for sinning. Rather than seeking redemptive means to restore them to God and others, these organizations seemed more about protecting the brand, keeping their team from contamination, and having no desire or competency to enter into the sinner's problems. The gospel came to draw us out by creating contexts of grace that encourage people to talk freely, transparently, and honestly about who they are and how they struggle.

The First Step

The first step in being free from sin is a confession— speaking the truth about what is wrong with us. If we struggle with hate toward anyone, we must talk to God first, asking Him to forgive us. Perhaps, afterward, we need to pursue reconciliation with that person. Listen to John.

> If we say we have no sin, we deceive ourselves, and the truth is not in us. If we confess our sins, he is faithful and just to forgive us our sins and to cleanse us from all unrighteousness. If we say we have not sinned, we make him a liar, and his word is not in us.
>
> (1 John 1:8-10)

It is not wise or appropriate to share your current sins with just anyone or everyone. There is no need to disseminate your sins with the world, but you should be in a context of competent helpers who can come alongside you to help you overcome the things that hinder you in your sanctification. The solution I'm suggesting is less about blaring your sins to the masses and more about being honest with a few people who can activate "one another-ing" in your life. What we must not do is condemn folks with no hope of them getting on a path to change. Problems have to lead to solutions, or those problems will metastasize into all sorts of complicating matters.

Honest Hindrances

Do you have folks with whom you can share your life with vulnerability and honesty? If you don't sense that freedom with your friends, start by assessing yourself. Are you doing something that hinders honesty? What are the things that distort an environment of grace in your relationships? How should you change? Start here before focusing on what others should do. Prejudice is just one of the many ways someone can say, "I don't like you."

If your goal is a redemptive-type activity in a person's life, you want to identify and remove whatever hindrances keep you from being that way with them. Whatever drives a wedge between you and others has a condemnation element. There is no sense of condemnation with the Lord (1 John 4:19). This news is good and releases you to come to Him with all your problems. God will accept and love you, and He will not condemn you. God will help you if you are honest with Him and you want to imitate Him to others (1 Corinthians 11:1).

> There is therefore now no condemnation for those who are in Christ Jesus.
>
> (Romans 8:1)

Name and Claim

The list of individuals we can struggle with is as long as the differences between people. Who is on your list? Can you love someone who has hurt you, disappointed you, or not met your expectations? I'm not asking you to become best mates, but if you cannot love them, what is your response to the Savior's words here?

> You have heard that it was said, "You shall love your neighbor and hate your enemy." But I say to you, Love your enemies and pray for those who persecute

you, so that you may be sons of your Father who
is in heaven. For he makes his sun rise on the evil
and on the good, and sends rain on the just and on
the unjust. For if you love those who love you, what
reward do you have? Do not even the tax collectors
do the same? And if you greet only your brothers,
what more are you doing than others? Do not even
the Gentiles do the same? You therefore must be
perfect, as your heavenly Father is perfect.

(Matthew 5:43-48)

- Do you dislike black people?
- What about gays?
- How about those who have had an abortion?
- Do you disdain feministic, egalitarian women?
- What about your spouse? Do you have uninterrupted
  love for your spouse?
- How about your parents?

There is a distinction between being against a person's
sinfulness and being against the person. I am talking about
the evil of disdaining certain types of people who are fellow
image-bearers. This concept is where the gospel should
have the highest inflection point in our hearts.

Call to Action

1. Can you be honest with another person or within
   a small group of friends about your sinfulness? If
   not, why not? Are they the right kind of friends for
   you?
2. Are there prejudices, bigotries, and other forms of
   self-righteousness that keep you from being like
   Jesus to all people? If so, will you do something
   about this for the gospel's sake?

6

Gun Control

When mass shootings happen, many rational and reasonable people stand on all sides of the gun control debate. Some folks want to limit the number of guns we have and how we use them. Others want to eliminate all guns. Then, some want more freedom regarding firearms. The debate is ongoing, but it always intensifies when there is a murder. These shootings rip out our hearts as we try to wrap our minds around what happened. It does not matter how many times you hear of it or how much violence you watch on television; when you hear a story about people killing people, the sadness begins to overwhelm you.

Cultural Evangelist

The initial response is to mourn. You grieve for the victims of the crime. You grieve for the families and friends of those who lost loved ones. You weep for a twisted individual who exchanged the truth of God for a lie. You struggle because the chattering class and political elites do not talk about God's solution. He is the only one who can reverse the curse of the evil one who scored another victory with another shooting. When a murder happens, every platform's news is a steady stream from every possible storyline, making it the perfect opportunity for the cultural evangelists to move the discussion into their corner. Why not? The senseless tragedy provides the pundits the platform to preach their gospel. Like any good cultural evangelist, they want to seize the moment. They are looking for converts. I do a similar thing.

When I write, I hope to grip and take you where I want you to go. I aim to show you Christ—the purpose of all my writings. The cultural evangelist's plan is similar but with different objectives and outcomes. The Bible is not their cherished presupposition or their hermeneutic. They begin with a heart-wrenching story and then launch into their politicized agenda. Gun control is one of those agendas, and every mass shooting presents the opportunity for them to pontificate. What strikes me about the gun control argument is how the storyline always moves from human responsibility to the fault of guns. If I didn't know what guns were, it would be easy to think they were free moral agents who exercised their will over humans. There are three ways the cultural evangelist communicates these ideas.

- **GUN VIOLENCE:** The cultural evangelists give an inanimate object life and agency to cause harm.
- **GUN MORALITY:** The cultural evangelists give an inanimate object morality—to choose good or evil.
- **GUN POWER:** The cultural evangelists give an inanimate object the power to bring hurt to someone.

Gun Violence?

The first shift in the argument is when the evangelist uses the term gun violence. This labeling is a subtle but astute change if you want to move the discussion from human responsibility to inanimate objects. Make them animated; it's the worldview difference between gun violence and human violence. This euphemistic maneuver happens when they make the weapon violent rather than the human wielding the weapon. You can do the same thing with sticks and stones; it's rock violence if I hit you with a rock. If I hit you over the head with a stick, it would be stick violence. This misdirection moves the potential cultural convert from thinking less about people and more about sticks, stones, and guns, which is more than semantics. It is an agenda.

It's a cultural worldview designed to shape policy. Once we put the accent mark on the gun rather than the sinner wielding the weapon, we've set ourselves up as secondary actors, passive aggressors, not primary culprits. The evangelist's argument is about guns, as though the person who slaughtered the people was not guilty of his actions. If you follow the logic, the solution is to incarcerate the gun (gun control) rather than the gunman. Of course, the progressive left does want to release more convicted criminals onto our streets. They want us to assume if you managed all inanimate objects capable of being used to hurt someone, you would solve the problem.

I do not fault unbelievers for pushing this agenda or expect an unbelieving media culture to put forth Christian values. Their argument is their worldview, and they cannot consider the doctrinal interplay between hamartiology, anthropology, and soteriology. They can't understand how violence does not come from a gun, but a sinful heart. The gun is an instrument that a violent person uses to carry out his violent actions. An inanimate object has no ability or power to harm anyone if a depraved soul chooses not to be the active agent in this nightmarish drama. A mass shooting is no different from the first recorded murder from this perspective. If the cultural evangelist argued the case back in Cain and Abel's day, he would push for rock control or stick control or whatever object Cain chose to kill his brother.

Cain spoke to Abel his brother. And when they were in the field, Cain rose up against his brother Abel and killed him.

(Genesis 4:8)

Gun Morality?

Thus, the possession of guns is the problem, and though I agree with them partly, I reject how they position the argument and the word choices to disguise the real issue. The cultural evangelists give an inanimate object morality. For example, "If the assailant did not own guns, the victims would be alive today." That might be true. I would never dismiss that kind of reasoning as though it is ludicrous or carries no validity. The problem I have is where the gun controllers place the weight of the argument. They move the issue to the gun without mentioning the real culprit. If the assailant survives, he will stand trial for this hate crime. His weapons would not.

There is only one culprit in this morality play: the assailant. He is the free moral agent who chooses to pick up an inanimate object and kill human beings. If they want to make a hypothetical argument by saying the assailant would not have killed if he had no gun, I could make an opposite argument, saying he would have killed them with something else, e.g., a machete. Both opinions (mine and theirs) are speculative and miss the point: this is more of a moral problem than a gun issue. When our children use an object to hurt one of their siblings, the thrust of my response to them is not about the thing used. I'm more interested in addressing the heart of the person who made a moral decision to hurt someone.

If God changes the child's heart, the objects around our home will not be weapons for destruction. Banning every possible thing that someone can use to hurt someone does not make sense when evil has gripped the hearts of fallen people. Because this is a moral argument, we do have a solution. But if the cultural evangelist gets his way by making it a gun argument, there is no solution, not until the government can control all possible objects that people can use to kill. Even if that were possible, there is still the matter of human depravity. If sinful people are not held accountable for their immoral actions, there is no possible way to control guns or any other weapon of choice.

Gun Power?

Handguns do not enhance our safety. They exacerbate our flaws, tempt us to escalate arguments, and bait us into embracing confrontation rather than avoiding it.

– Cultural Evangelist

Initially, the evangelists talk about the violence of the gun, not the man wielding it. Then, they placed morality on the gun rather than the man. Lastly, they give the weapon the ability to gaslight a human being. Guns can cause us to sin by exacerbating, tempting, and baiting us to pick them up and shoot someone. James debunked this argument long ago when he addressed the source of our anger. These two verses read as though they came out of today's newspaper. According to James, the gun did not tempt, exacerbate, or bait the killer to kill. He murdered because there was something he wanted but could not get, so he chose to murder.

What causes quarrels and what causes fights among you? Is it not this, that your passions are at war within you? You desire and do not have, so you murder. You covet and cannot obtain, so you fight and quarrel.

(James 4:1-2)

Saying guns tempt us is a common mistake. We all have done this. How often have you gotten angry and justified your anger by blaming something outside of yourself for the offense? Any time we look beyond ourselves to explain the cause of our anger, we are no longer walking in the truth (James 1:14-16). Though I appreciate anyone's desire to curb violence and make our culture a safer place to live, if we try to bring in social change while dismissing God's Word, we are deceiving ourselves, and the excellent desire we may want for society will never happen.

Moving the storyline from appropriate mourning over the senseless deaths of people made in the image of God to the primary cause of those murders being something other than human responsibility is misguided and unproductive. Guns have no life, morality, or power, but people do. The issue is that the human vs. gun argument should not be an either/or debate. There is truth on both sides. The cultural evangelist is making it a one-sided view—the problem is with the gun. I gave a counter-argument—the primary concern is not with the gun. If the culture ever turns the argument back to the people behind the weapons, they would be in a better place for resolution.

Let's Talk

But I would not want to leave you thinking there is no problem with guns. There is. If our child abused a sibling with an inanimate object, I would deal with their heart first. Then, I would make sure there were rules to mitigate the possibility of it happening again. For example, it would be unwise for me to put boxes of BBs on the kitchen counter for a child to act out their evil heart perchance they wanted to hurt someone. That misguidedness would be foolish parenting because I would not be thinking through the doctrine of sin present in our child's heart. The answer is not legalism (absolutely no guns) or licentiousness (total gun freedom).

I believe the murder rate could go down if there were stricter practices and policies regarding firearms, especially for those with criminal records. My point is not to say enacting policies won't work. God gave us policies because of our hard hearts (Matthew 19:8). Policies can work to a degree, but the real issue will always be with human responsibility versus hard-heartedness. We should have a more productive dialogue regarding the main problem rather than shifting the discussion to lesser or specious arguments.

It would be more effective if our cultural evangelists wrote about moral issues like parenting, fatherless homes, firearm responsibility, heart issues, and objective, statistical demographics that are more likely to kill someone. I do hear you, cultural evangelists. I'm not going to leave a gun readily available for our immature child to pick up and use willy-nilly. I'm willing to embrace your worldview to a point. Let's talk about being responsible with guns. But do you hear me? Will you embrace my worldview that this is primarily a human morality problem?

Call to Action

1. What's your take on the gun control argument? Using the Bible as your primary source, will you make a case for what you believe?
2. Are you aware of the gun violence statistics? Where do most killings take place? What are some of the common denominators? What solutions would you like to see?
3. Which demographics are safer, and what are a few reasons for it?
4. How active are you culturally? Are you gathering, processing, and understanding the data? What should your role be in engaging the culture from a bibliocentric worldview?
5. If you have children, how are you indoctrinating them about the cause of sin, e.g., anger? What does walking out repentance look like in your life?
6. Are they tempted to blame outside sources as the cause of their anger? Do you?

7

Donald Trump

One of the striking surprises about the time we live is the imperceptible and incremental changes that happen culturally. Things move so slowly, and we're so preoccupied that we don't recognize shifts until we're shocked out of our quiet and mundane lives. The evolution of marketing and politics is one of those phenomena of our society that leaped forward in 2015. What happened is a stark call to action for all believers who love their country and want to make a positive, redemptive difference in the lives of others.

Enter Kennedy

On September 26, 1960, the timeline for politics changed forever after John F. Kennedy and Richard Nixon squared off for the first-ever nationally televised political debate. The handsome but relatively unknown Kennedy was going up against the political machine and seasoned warhorse Richard M. Nixon. This event was supposed to be a quick night's work for Nixon. Kennedy was not even his dad's first choice to be the first Catholic President of the United States, but it fell to him after the death of his elder brother.

By the end of the sixty-minute time-limited match between these two combatants, Nixon was sprawled out on the mat unconscious, hyperbolically speaking. At the same time, Kennedy became the new heavyweight champion of the world. It was on that night the political season was over, and what was going to happen a few weeks later on election day in November was anti-climatic. Here is how Time magazine reflected on that history-changing event on its 50th anniversary:

> On the morning of September 26, 1960, John F. Kennedy was a relatively unknown senator from Massachusetts. He was young and Catholic—neither of which helped his image—and facing off against an incumbent. But by the end of the evening, he was a star.
>
> It's now common knowledge that without the nation's first televised debate—fifty years ago Sunday—Kennedy would never have been President. But beyond securing his presidential career, the 60-minute duel between the handsome Irish-American senator and Vice President Richard Nixon fundamentally altered political campaigns, television media, and America's political history.
>
> It's one of those unusual points on the timeline of history where you can say things changed very dramatically—in this case, in a single night, says Alan Schroeder, a media historian and associate professor at Northeastern University, who authored the book, *Presidential Debates: Forty Years of High-Risk TV.*
>
> — Time Magazine

Sight vs. Sound

The two things Kennedy understood (or stumbled into) were the medium and the mind of the American public. Though nobody could tell you today what they debated, everyone who watched it could tell you what they saw. The sweating, stammering Nixon, who was recovering from a recent stay in the hospital, cowered under the bright lights while the calm, cool, and collected Kennedy seemed to tower over his opponent as the seconds ticked by. What they were saying became less important than how they presented themselves until it didn't matter any longer that Kennedy was a Catholic, too young, and didn't have enough experience.

It also didn't matter that Nixon had spent his entire adult life in the political arena dusting off foe after foe. Sitting next to Dwight D. Eisenhower for eight years was not enough political credibility to carry the election. 1960 was a transitional point. The percentage of Americans owning televisions jumped from 11% the year before to 88% when the debate aired. A bright, shiny, almost omnipresent experience was sitting in our living rooms, where we could watch the world like never before. I realize it is hard for us to imagine the power of television because our ubiquitous friend has always been one of our favorite family members, babysitters, diversionary strategists, worldview sculptors, and sleep agents. Not so in 1960. It was a first-time event.

Imagine seeing the Grand Canyon for the first time. You walk to the rim and look over. Then you look to the left and right. As far as the eye will travel, there is no end to its wonder. Then you try to capture in a word what the eye is straining to see—the right word. You can't. Years later, you may not remember the details of your vacation, but you'll never forget that time you first looked over the rim. That was the television in 1960. Kennedy embraced the medium in September and narrowly beat the old warhorse in November. We had a new president, and television became the marketing means of choice to persuade the masses. Instructively, most of the people who listened to the debate on the radio thought Nixon had won. The lesson is that sight is more persuasive than sound or substance.

Enter Trump

Donald J. Trump is the second coming of John F. Kennedy from a political and marketing perspective. He took what John Kennedy did to a new, surreal level in 2015. Kennedy's generation buried their heads in books and their ears tuned to a radio. Trump's generation reads far fewer books but spends excessive time watching television or hanging out in their favorite social media communities. You can pick any random stat about TV viewing, and it will always be more than other mediums. One New York Daily News report said the average American watches over five hours daily. That is a staggering number, considering the average American does not read for five hours daily. The shaping influences provided by the people behind the TV camera have been in full swing for over fifty years.

To what degree Donald Trump knows this, I do not know. I know he is the primary political figure who knows how to act out what we have grown accustomed to seeing in the movies and television. Think hyperbole. Think WWE—World Wrestling Entertainment. Donald Trump is WWE personified. He is not real—in that sense. He's an over-the-top entertainer who entered the political arena, a fictitious Marvel movie played out on the political stage. He's a WWE character whooping it up before the masses. Do you know why professional wrestling has been so historically popular for decades? It's vicarious.

Wrestling is the arena where you can watch live hyperbolic action heroes do what we can't do—beat up other people. Whether it makes the fan feel affirmed to see good triumph over evil or the grappling lets off a bit of mundane steam, wrestling has proven to persuade the will of the masses. In the early days of wrestling, good triumphed over evil, but over the last few decades, even the villains have been celebrated because they are given better storylines. The scripts between good and evil are so blurred that no one discerns or cares. It's not about who they are or their virtues but how they perform.

The New Medium

Donald Trump knows how to embrace the debate stage. In 2015, Jeb Bush looked lost fumbling around on stage. The only thing we remember about Trump and Hillary is that he threatened to put her in jail. The one-and-only debate between Trump and Biden in the summer of 2024 was a no-contest. Joe Biden was Richard Nixon all over again, but far worse due to his dementia. The script has changed, and the viewing audience is different. Donald knows it's not a political debate. He is marketing as much as he is doing the work of politicking. I'm not assessing his motives because I have no idea what they are. I'm stating that Donald Trump has adapted his message to today's high-octane medium and resonates like no other political figure has since Ronald Reagan. Imagine these kinds of debates in 1960. They would have been replaced with sixty minutes of non-stop commercials or clips of Elvis from the waist up.

Donald Trump is entertaining to a large portion of America because he says things that a pent-up and angry culture has been saying from a smaller stage for decades. The person who taps into the American consciousness on a grand scale will be hard to beat. "Who cares what he's saying!" That's not a question searching for an answer or a statement up for debate. "He's saying it like it is. That's exactly what I think about our political system." When an entertainment medium (WWE) can motivate grown men to paint their faces and yell obscenities in front of their children in a public venue, why are you surprised that the political medium can capture the mind of the politically frustrated to where it does not matter who the person is as long as they feel vicariously vindicated or affirmed?

Uneasy Pragmatism

As a pragmatic supporter of Donald Trump, my endorsement of his presidency is rooted in a calculated assessment rather than personal admiration. While I acknowledge the positive aspects of some of his policies, I am profoundly aware of the numerous character flaws that make him a contentious figure. My support stems from a pragmatic analysis of the current political landscape, where the available choices necessitate focusing on policy outcomes over personal virtues.

Donald Trump is undeniably a product of the media age, where optics, marketing, and public persona wield a significant influence over public perception. His presence in the political arena has been shaped by a media environment prioritizing sensationalism over substance, contributing to the polarization and spectacle defining modern politics. This media-driven dynamic has elevated Trump to a position where his personality often overshadows the content of his policies, making it challenging to reconcile his public behavior with the gravity of the office he has held and might hold again.

My reservations about Trump are substantial and multifaceted. He has demonstrated a pattern of behavior that includes multiple instances of adultery, crude remarks, pettiness, and a general disposition that often appears at odds with the decorum and dignity expected of the President of the United States. These character flaws are not trivial; they reflect a broader cultural shift towards the normalization of debauchery and a decline in leadership standards. Trump's conduct is emblematic of a political class that has devolved into degeneracy, power hunger, and greed, creating a landscape where candidates like him can thrive.

He's a Symptom

My pragmatic approach reflects a broader trend in contemporary politics where the criteria for voting centers increasingly on policy pragmatics rather than the personal virtues of candidates. The degradation of the political class has created a scenario where voters are often faced with choosing the lesser of two evils, focusing on practical outcomes over ideal leadership qualities. With all its flaws, Trump's presidency highlights the urgent need for us to reevaluate the standards and expectations we hold for our leaders. In essence, Donald Trump is a symptom, not a cause, of the current state of American politics.

His rise to power underscores the deep-seated issues within the political system that have allowed for the normalization of behavior previously deemed unacceptable for public office. As a pragmatic supporter, my vote for Trump is not an endorsement of his character but a strategic decision to achieve policy objectives in a flawed political environment that shows more concern for manipulating clicks, censoring the dissenter, and gaslighting the masses into passive subjugation. This perspective necessitates a sober recognition of the limitations and challenges of the current political landscape, where pragmatism often takes precedence over idealism in the pursuit of governance.

We are all guilty of where we are today. We have embraced the new medium and refuse to step away from our social toys. Donald Trump and his political ilk would not have been our ubiquitous entertainers if we had made different choices. It was not all Kennedy's fault that millions sat enthralled and enamored with the medium. He stepped into it and gave us what we wanted. Based on the growing power of social media, it's easy to understand why we have Donald Trump. I pray that we recognize what we're doing to ourselves and make proactive changes before the next culture shift comes along and a worse-than-Trump steps into it to lead us to where only God knows.

Call to Action

1. Everything changes, but not always for our good and God's fame. As you reflect on this chapter, what changes can you make to stem the political and cultural tide?
2. It would be worth doing some life over coffee with a friend, thinking about how you have contributed to the current state of affairs.
3. I like to think about the redemptive use of technology as the counter-thought to this new medium that gave rise to our cultural and political class. Perhaps reflecting on how you can use technology for God's fame would be an excellent place to focus.

8

Presidential Election

Every four years in America, its citizens have the opportunity to vote for the next President of the United States. It's the privilege of free countries where the political class serves the citizens, or that is what it says on paper. In America, it's no longer that way in practice as the government has become the hegemonic power, making the right to vote a fragile and sober time when faith and responsibility intersect at a high level.

Like a Foreigner

To vote for a national leader is an honor in the United States. Though it's self-evident, knowing that citizens from other countries do not have that privilege. Voting is something that I do not take for granted. Though there are many problematic issues in our nation, being able to vote for a president is one of the better things. The privilege of voting for a leader is a reminder for Christians because our Americanism is not the essential thing that describes who we are. Living in America and being an American is like having a temporary visa because of our alien status. America is not our permanent address; we have an other-worldly and life-altering citizenship.

But our citizenship is in heaven, and from it we await a Savior, the Lord Jesus Christ (Philippians 3:20). By faith he went to live in the land of promise, as in a foreign land, living in tents with Isaac and Jacob, heirs with him of the same promise. For he was looking forward to the city that has foundations, whose designer and builder is God.

(Hebrews 11:9-10)

Christians live as though they are in a foreign country. Like Abraham, our Old Testament brother, God has called some of His children to live in America for His fame. We live on American soil with our tents, but not as people with deep roots. We are waiting on the Lord to take us to a better place as we live out this chapter before that glorious exodus. When the good Lord calls us to our permanent, eternal home, we will gladly kiss this place goodbye and follow Him to the land of promise.

Our presupposition shapes our worldview regarding our temporary existence on Earth, which is why our hearts are not unduly troubled by an upcoming election. As a responsible citizen in my temporary home, I will cast my vote. I will ask the Lord to accomplish His perfect will, and I will rest in my Lord, which is one of the many perks of being in His family. I trust these potent words from our Leader will settle your soul as you think about the election season and the outcome.

Let not your hearts be troubled. Believe in God; believe also in me. In my Father's house are many rooms. If it were not so, would I have told you that I go to prepare a place for you? And if I go and prepare a place for you, I will come again and will take you to myself, that where I am you may be also.

(John 14:1-3)

Good Stewards

One way to think about living as a foreigner in a foreign land is to consider yourself on vacation. You go on vacation for a few days or weeks. If it's a great one, you're okay with extending it. For those of us who have had horrible life experiences or are nearing the end of our lives, we look forward to entering into the Lord's rest. But while on vacation, you act responsibly. You don't steal the towels or the Bibles during your hotel stay. You want to be Jesus everywhere you go, even while vacationing. But it's never lost on you that it's not your home. You have a permanent residence and long to be there when the vacation ends. Christians are responsible for making God's name great because believers do not divorce themselves from who they are, no matter where they live. We are Christlike examples who hope that our sphere of influence will observe and follow us (Ephesians 5:1; 1 Corinthians 11:1).

We are stewards of God's blessings all the time. This worldview is why Christians see their local and national responsibilities through a biblical filter. We want to do our duty as temporary citizens by modeling and practicing stewardship opportunities. We are stewards of this gift of life, and casting a vote is one way to steward the sober responsibility of being a permanent Christian in temporary America. I vote because I care about my temporary alien residence. While I'm a sovereigntist by practice, I also believe in human responsibility. I'm comfortable living in the mystery of these two truths (Deuteronomy 29:29). Believers live in that space between God's sovereign control over all things and our responsibility to vote (Genesis 50:20).

Voting Memories

Lucia and I have passed this stewardship vision to our children. When they were younger, they went with us to the voting place. We made it a family event. They did not fully understand the process but loved being with us, standing in the long, curvy lines, and chatting up our neighbors. Typically, we would take pastries to the poll volunteers and thank them for their sacrifice by serving us. Our kids loved the voting stickers. I hoped the process of voting would be one of the many ways our children would think about stewarding the Lord's mercies to them. When our oldest came of age, she followed our lead by casting her ballot. Not every person gets a chance to cast a vote for a temporary leader of their temporary home.

A Candidate Dilemma

In most presidential elections, two leading candidates are running for office. Typically, neither candidate carries an authentic Christian message or fully embraces our Christian values. In most cases, a candidate's pragmatism is the vital thing: "I'll take the position that will give me the most votes." Authentic Christian candidates tend to get shouted down or marginalized when it comes to the popular vote. I would not expect anything else in a paganized country where the centrality of Christ is a target for mocking rather than a reality that calls for our highest praises. When it comes to politics, little has changed throughout human history. If Christ were running for office in His day, I'm sure the power brokers would have doubled down to ensure that He would not ascend to a political position of power. Typically, our candidates either reject God altogether or marginally acknowledge Him, which always raises the question among some Christians, "How can you vote for a nonbeliever?"

Affirming Non-Christians

The question is odd in light of our affirmation of many non-Christian people and things. We cast our ballots, affirm organizations, give money, and support unbelievers' causes regularly. It's a common practice for Christians. To live in this world, you cannot do otherwise. What is one of your favorite movies? All of them aren't Christian flicks. What about a popular leader, entertainer, or athlete who does not align with your ethics? You do not have to feel guilty about participating or enjoying something from a fellow image-bearer who happens to be a pagan. God's common grace does rain on unjust people (Matthew 5:45). There are times when some pagan people use their gifts so that a Christian can support them. You should not have a conscience issue about voting for an unregenerate person who lines up better with your Christian values than another unbeliever. Of course, you can refrain from voting if it's a conscience issue for you. However, how does not participating square with your call to be salt and light in your world (Matthew 5:13-16)?

God's Man

The king's heart is a stream of water in the hand of the LORD; he turns it wherever he will.

(Proverbs 21:1)

For the Scripture says to Pharaoh, "For this very purpose I have raised you up, that I might show my power in you, and that my name might be proclaimed in all the earth."

(Romans 9:17)

These are two controlling verses that I find comfort in regarding national elections. They also help to guard my heart against anger, worry, anxiety, or fear. If these verses are new to you, perhaps you can add them to your toolbox to protect your soul against temptations. God will have His person in the office. Become a good sovereigntist when it comes to elections. You're not dismissing your personal responsibility but want to find your sweet spot between those two doctrinal responsibilities. Are you comfortable living in that mystery? Of course, you know there is a logical priority regarding sovereignty and responsibility. Though you live in the mystery, you know the Sovereign Lord is always first in your theology and practice.

Primary and Secondary

This Jesus, delivered up according to the definite plan and foreknowledge of God, you crucified and killed by the hands of lawless men.

(Acts 2:23)

Notice how Peter thought about these two doctrines while preaching in Acts, as he brought these realities together. He merged God's definite plan to crucify His Son and the responsible people who delivered Jesus as part of the Lord's redemptive purposes. Peter was talking about primary and secondary causes. God is always the primary cause, while fully responsible humans are the secondary causes who cooperate with God in the story that the Lord is writing. Though you have the opportunity to do something, you can simultaneously rest, knowing that God is always in control. If your candidate does not get into office, you continue to situate your faith in the Sovereign Lord rather than the candidate of your choice. This season is not a time for anxiousness or anger, not if you're a Christian. This political opportunity is a time for the people of faith to demonstrate to the world what true worship is when practically applied.

85

A Lousy President

Maybe God will raise a lousy president to make His name great. It won't be the first time He did this. I have wondered what folks thought about Pharaoh rising to national political prominence during the time of Egyptian world power. I don't think I would have voted for him. I would have hoped for Moses to rule. But God chose another man because He had a better plan (Isaiah 55:8-9). Reflect on these two thoughts as you think about a potential ungodly president at the helm of our country.

- You could fret while responding with sinful anger.
- You could let the world see that you've situated your faith in the knowledge that God is in control even if your candidate does not win (Romans 9:17).

I pray you will vote and show your faith in God, even if your candidate does not get into office. You can do this because you are a Christian, and you know at some level of your heart that human strategies or the devil's schemes will not thwart God's plans (1 Corinthians 1:25).

Guard, and Pray Often

One of the curiosities about Christians and politics is the lack of faith that some of them exhibit. Hearing faith-filled responses from Christians during a political cycle is becoming rare. Too many Christians sound similar to the secular culture in their snarkiness, frustration, and fretting. When believers get involved in politics, god-centered courage and compassion are not the norm. It's sad. If you were to put all the Christian comments about politics and politicians in the same basket as the world's speech, it would be a challenge to tell the difference.

Let your speech always be gracious, seasoned with salt, so that you may know how you ought to answer each person.

(Colossians 4:6)

We should involve ourselves in our country's cultural and political happenings, but we should do it with faith and grace rather than thinking, talking, and acting like our worldly counterparts. When it comes to politics, some Christians seem to be more under the spell of the harsh talking heads in the chattering class than the illuminating and controlling power of the Spirit of God. You don't have to vote for those who are against some of the things you value the most, and you don't have to speak unkindly or derogatory about those candidates. They are people made in the image of God (Genesis 1:26-27). They do not need our sinful anger or our hatred. They need our Jesus. I suspect we will never agree with their politics or agendas, but we can pray for them.

With [our tongues], we bless our Lord and Father, and with it, we curse people who are made in the likeness of God.

(James 3:9)

Call to Action

As you prepare to vote, please check the "God-centered box" in your heart first. Will you vote for God's control over you while resting in His will? Christians will ultimately win. And since you know the outcome already, let's be gracious ultimate winners while seeking to make the name of our Candidate look great among those who don't know Him.

Eight Planks of My Political Platform

1. America is not my home. I'm a stranger passing through this land.
2. I love my temporal country and will do my part to make it better.
3. My eschatological view teaches me to be okay if things don't go my way.
4. I will fulfill my responsibility, but my faith is elsewhere (Luke 22:42).
5. Regardless of who wins, I will continue to tell others about Jesus.
6. I will pray for our President, no matter who it is (Proverbs 21:1).
7. I trust the Sovereign Lord to care for everything, including elections.
8. I will be a gracious ultimate victor while waiting for my permanent residence.

9

Conclusion

The gospel practicalized is a transcendent lifestyle that overrides cultural, political, and religious traditions, preferences, and expectations. The convolution between primary and secondary things can be dizzying, especially in a world that works overtime to invert what is good with evil. A practicalized gospel teaches us to live well with others, especially those who make choices that are different from ours. In a world gone mad, all Christians must work hard to distinguish the negotiable from the non-negotiable.

Different Strokes

Working through preferential, secondary issues is like wrestling a greased pig: you can't get your arms around them all, and just when you think you have a good grasp on the essential things, something changes. Our part of the country does [fill in the blank], and another part of the country does it differently. This family believes [such-and-such] is correct, while the next family does the opposite.

- Should I say "in Jesus' name" at the end of all my prayers?
- Can I drink a beer?
- Is it wrong to have lost friends?
- Should I agree with everything my church is doing?
- Why did he vote for that person?

Then, there is the generational struggle. The old guard is perplexed by the ubiquitous control and manipulation of technology, while the new guard drinks technology like spiked water, living with it as though it were an addictive appendage. The older you get, the more you feel like the "get off my lawn" guy as you sing along with Bob Dylan about how the times are 'a-changin'."

> *Come gather 'round people*
> *Wherever you roam*
> *And admit that the waters*
> *Around you have grown*
> *And accept it that soon*
> *You'll be drenched to the bone*
> *If your time to you*
> *Is worth savin'*
> *Then you better start swimmin'*
> *Or you'll sink like a stone*
> *For the times they are a-changin'.*

Gospel Priority

Because of the myriad of preferences, desires, and false assumptions, wisdom recognizes it's best not to make cultural or religious preferences the primary point of focus or normative while choosing to learn how to live out the practicalities of the gospel as first importance—the main thing. The gospel practicalized is a transcendent lifestyle that rises above our cultural and religious traditions, preferences, and expectations. The more adept you are at making these gospel applications, the less soul noise you'll experience in a world that makes a living shouting at each other.

Christ is our glorious example of someone who was willing to obey the customs of His day, and for the most part, He did follow those customs unless they negatively impacted the higher purposes of the gospel. Learning how to live Christlike regarding secondary matters is the goal for all believers. Here is a five-step, sequential process that works in a transformative progression that loosens the Christian from the control of secondary issues. These steps are essential and non-negotiable if you want to experience transformation from the inside out and enabled to love others well, especially those who do things differently from you.

- **STEP 1:** The gospel teaches that we all are mutually depraved and equally in need of a great Savior. Mercifully, God came to each of us—who are born from above—and gave us the gift of salvation. This gift of salvation has many elements: faith, repentance, justification, adoption, definitive sanctification, etc.
- **STEP 2:** After God regenerates us, our inner person begins a renewal process by the power of the gospel (Ephesians 4:23). We call this lifelong, evolving process progressive sanctification, where we indeed mature incrementally, much like a child growing from infancy to adulthood.
- **STEP 3:** The doctrines of salvation and sanctification are humbling doctrines. Together, they remind us of our helplessness apart from the gospel's rescuing and restoring. Correctly understanding our salvation and sanctification humbles us.
- **STEP 4:** James 4:6 promises that the humble person will receive God's empowering favor, which enables the Christian to change, grow, and mature. This process enables us to love others, including loving hard-to-love people.
- **STEP 5:** 1 Corinthians 13:4-8 provides a list of love actions that we can apply to our relationships. Read this list by inserting your name each time love is mentioned or implied.

1. _____ is patient.
2. _____ is kind.
3. _____ does not envy.
4. _____ does not boast.
5. _____ is not arrogant.
6. _____ is not rude.
7. _____ does not insist on his/her own way.
8. _____ is not irritable.
9. _____ is not resentful.
10. _____ does not rejoice at wrongdoing.
11. _____ rejoices with the truth.
12. _____ bears all things.
13. _____ believes all things.
14. _____ hopes all things.
15. _____ endures all things.

The love list merely samples how a gospel-motivated person operates in God's world. A gospelized person can love others expansively because of Christ's strength operating in them (Philippians 4:13). This empowerment makes the gospel (Christ) the base for and point of departure when considering how to live with others who have different preferences.

Gospel Logic

- Gospel + Transformation = Humility
- Humility + Empowering Grace = God-centered love actions—the ability to love others who are different.

The danger of not following this gospel formula can make your preferences an undeviating mandate, which will more than likely make what you prefer a yoke of bondage around your friend's necks. Understanding the power of legalistic preferences and the practicalization of the gospel to offset rules and traditions is crucial. The gospel trains and equips us to experience its transformative power rather than managing our unique-to-us preferences.

- Is the goal in our relationships to control them with our set of secondary rules?
- Or would we prefer to lead them into a deeper, practicalized understanding of the gospel that frees them to decide what's best for them regarding secondary issues?

The former will bind their consciences into lifelong bondage and possibly future rebellion. The latter will hopefully teach them how to change, grow, and mature—all within the power and parameters of the gospel. Without the gospel, our friends will learn preferences by rote, context, and culture. The New Testament equivalent to this was the Pharisees. They codified the rules without deviation or sound apologetics. In time, their religion became a joyless, fear-based, hollow, and mandated set of rules that made them out of sync with the culture they were supposed to evangelize.

Gospel Keys

The gospel is more pneumatic than top-down rigid rules. Gospel people are not afraid to penetrate their culture, choosing to become all things to all people while praying that God will win some of them to Himself. Two extreme worldviews adulterate this gospel objective:

- Those who separate from the world, which stifles the gospel.
- Those who imbibe the world, which also stifles the gospel.

Christ did not separate or imbibe. He penetrated the culture, became connected to, sympathized with, and helped them change without being distant, afraid, self-righteous, or compromised. Perhaps these six gospel keys will help you assess how well you engage others who believe differently from you.

1. **REGENERATED:** Are you born again?
2. **AFFECTION:** How would you describe your affection for the gospel?
3. **LOVE OTHERS:** Are you managed by a desire to love others, or do their preferences manage you?
4. **ENGAGE OTHERS:** Do you approach others out of a heart of love?
5. **ADAPT TO OTHERS:** Do you adapt to other people's preferences without compromising the gospel? Do you know how to adapt without compromising the gospel?
6. **WIN OTHERS:** Will you compromise your preferences for the sake of the gospel?

Here are the questions simplified:

1. *Regenerated +*
2. *Affection +*
3. *Love Others +*
4. *Engage Others +*
5. *Adapt to Others =*
6. *Win Others.*

Gospel Illustrated

When our kids were younger, our family would visit the Biltmore Estate in Asheville, North Carolina. It's a massive, sprawling, beautiful place with so much to see and do, in addition to touring the Biltmore mansion. One of our favorite things was to visit the winery on the estate. On one occasion, we invited some of our conservative friends, who are very close to us. Our children had sleepovers with their children and vice-versa. We love this family, and they have an anti-alcohol stance.

In overly simplistic, religious terms, you might consider them legalists, and we would be the pejorative liberals. Before our Biltmore visit, we sat down with our children to discuss discretion regarding preferences in the context of loving others who differ from us on secondary matters. The bottom line was that we would not go to the winery or even mention its existence while with our friends. Time in the winery was secondary to loving this family.

> Now concerning food offered to idols: we know that "all of us possess knowledge." This "knowledge" puffs up, but love builds up. If anyone imagines that he knows something, he does not yet know as he ought to know. But if anyone loves God, he is known by God.
>
> (1 Corinthians 8:1-3)

Our children were stellar. We enjoyed our friends while not making a secondary issue like the winery a point for division. I suspect they have had similar discussions about our lifestyle choices with their children. It is impossible to be in 100% agreement with everyone. Fortunately, you do not have to make a lock-step agreement essential for relating and engaging with others. This grace gift from the Lord is one of the things that sets Christians apart. We can be the aggressors when it comes to relating to those who are different from us.

Call to Action

The gospel does not demand that you have an eclectic friend list, but it should free you to engage with and enjoy those who do things differently from you. Isn't this why we love Jesus so much? We were not like Him, but He entered our world, hoping to engage, befriend, and transform some of us.

1. Do you intentionally relate to those who are different from you? What does being salt and light in the culture look like for you?
2. Are you more afraid of the influence of others; thus, you separate from them, or are you more determined to influence those who differ from you with the practical message of the gospel?
3. Culture and politics are the most divisive contexts in our world today. The easy thing to do is separate from those who choose differently from us. In light of this practical temptation, what should "being Jesus to the world" look like for you? Perhaps a time of life over coffee to discuss these matters with a friend would prove wise and transformative.

Live in harmony with one another. Do not be haughty, but associate with the lowly. Never be wise in your own sight.

(Romans 12:16)

About the Author

Rick Thomas launched the Life Over Coffee global training network in 2008 to bring hope and help for you and others by creating resources that spark conversations for transformation. His primary responsibilities are resource creation and leadership development, which he does through speaking, writing, podcasting, and educating. In 1990 he earned a BA in Theology and, in 1991, a BS in Education. In 1993, he received his ordination into Christian ministry, and in 2000, he graduated with an MA in Counseling from The Master's University. In 2006, he was recognized as a Fellow of the Association of Certified Biblical Counselors (ACBC).

Other Books Available from
Life Over Coffee

Boasting in Weakness
Centering Your Marriage on Christ
Communication
Complete Marriage
Don't Apologize
Exchange the Truth for a Lie
Help My Marriage Has Grown Cold
Identity Crisis
Local Church
Loving Me
Mad
Marriage Devotion We Are One
Politics and Culture
Parenting Devotion from Zero to Adulthood
Sex, Temptation, and Modesty
Storm Hurler
The Cyber Effect
The Talk
Wives Leading
You Decide

www.ingramcontent.com/pod-product-compliance
Lightning Source LLC
Chambersburg PA
CBHW071533120626
46550CB00006B/2447